Jane Goodall
and the Chimpanzees

Betsey Chessen • Pamela Chanko

Scholastic Inc.
New York • Toronto • London • Auckland • Sydney

Acknowledgments

Literacy Specialist: Linda Cornwell

Social Studies Consultant: Barbara Schubert, Ph.D.

Design: Silver Editions

Photo Research: Silver Editions

Endnotes: Elizabeth Scholl

Endnote Illustrations: Anthony Carnabucia

Photographs: Cover: Karl Ammann/Corbis; pp. 1, 12: Franck Spooner/Gamma Liaison; pp. 2, 3, 8, 10, 11, 13: Michael K. Nichols/National Geographic Society Image Collection; pp. 4, 6: Kenneth Love/National Geographic Society Image Collection; p. 5: Thomas White/ Gamma Liaison; p. 7: B. Rieger/Gamma Liaison; p. 9: Laguna Photo/Gamma Liaison.

Library of Congress Cataloging-in-Publication Data
Chessen, Betsey, 1970-
Jane Goodall and the chimpanzees/Betsey Chessen, Pamela Chanko.
p.cm. --(Social studies emergent readers)
summary: Simple text and photographs follow zoologist
Jane Goodall as she studies and records information about chimpanzees.
ISBN 0-439-04576-2 (pbk.: alk. paper)
1. Chimpanzees--Pictorial works--Juvenile literature. 2. Goodall, Jane, 1934- --Pictorial works--Juvenile literature.
[1. Chimpanzees. 2. Goodall, Jane, 1934-. 3. Zoologists.] I. Chanko, Pamela, 1968-. II. Title. III. Series.
QL737.P96C4724 1999
599.885'022'2--dc21   98-53335
                                                                        CIP AC

4   5   6   7   8   9   10   08   03   02   01   00   99

How does Jane study chimpanzees?

She asks questions about them

and watches closely.

She gathers information

and watches closely.

She records information

and watches closely.

She communicates

and watches closely.

She asks more questions

and watches closely.

Jane watches closely because she cares

Jane Goodall and the Chimpanzees

Jane Goodall was born in London, England, on April 3, 1934. As a child, Jane's love of and interest in animals began to unfold. When Jane read a book about an animal doctor called *The Story of Dr. Dolittle*, she decided she would surely go to Africa someday. Dr. Dolittle lived in Africa and had the ability to talk to the animals.

Years later Jane was invited to visit a friend in Kenya. Once in Africa, Jane met Dr. Louis Leakey, a world-famous researcher who was digging up bones of animals that lived millions of years ago. He asked Jane if she wanted a job studying a group of chimpanzees.

Jane could not believe it. This was like a dream come true. In 1960, at age 26, Jane arrived at the chimpanzee reserve in Tanzania. Before long, Jane felt as if she belonged there. She learned her way around the area and found places the chimpanzees visited each day. Jane spent long days in the forest with a small amount of food, a camera, and a notebook. Little by little, she and the chimpanzees became used to one another.

About a year after Jane arrived at the chimpanzee reserve, a photographer named Hugo Van Lawick was sent there by the National Geographic Society to make a film of Jane and the chimpanzees. Jane married Hugo, and they had a son nicknamed Grub.

For years Jane studied the chimpanzees in Tanzania. She then decided to broaden her work with chimpanzees. She was concerned with the welfare and survival of chimps all over the world.

Jane Goodall founded the Jane Goodall Institute for Wildlife Research, Education and Conservation in 1977 to provide ongoing support for field research on wild chimpanzees and to help stop the rapid decline of chimpanzee populations in the wild and neglect and abuse in captivity. Since then the Institute has expanded its mission to include conservation and environmental education, reforestation projects, and natural resource management.

The Jane Goodall Institute promotes wildlife research of primates in general and chimpanzees in particular, education efforts to heighten global awareness of the issues facing wild and captive chimpanzees, conservation activities to ensure the long-term preservation of the chimpanzee habitat, and animal welfare activities to ensure the physical and psychological well-being of animals in general, particularly chimpanzees.

In 1991 the Jane Goodall Institute established Roots & Shoots, an environmental education and humanitarian program for youth (preschool through university level). The mission of Roots & Shoots is to foster respect and compassion for all living things, promote understanding of all cultures and beliefs, and inspire each individual to take action to make the world a better place for animals, the environment, and the human community.

In order to become a member of the Roots & Shoots program, please contact:

Deputy of Roots & Shoots at the Jane Goodall Institute
1-800-592-JANE

Jane Goodall Institute
P.O. Box 14890
Silver Spring, MD 20911-4890
E-mail: janegoodall@wcsu.ctstateu.edu